Midnight Tears

Dr. R. Sam Koopman, BA; PhD

ISBN: 978-0-620-94092-4

DEDICATION

This work is dedicated to my firstborn Son Darian Miguel Samuel whom I love with all my heart.
You're my strength, my motivation and inspiration to reach higher. Daddy love you and I can't wait to see you again.

TABLE OF CONTENTS

THANKS

I wish to express my thanks to God in Heaven who warmly accepts our loved ones in the perfect Mansion that the Lord Jesus prepared for us.
Second, every person, here and above who encouraged, supported, criticized and ostracized me during my deepest moments of pain and suffering.
Professor Ed Van Den Bergh for honoring means doing the Preface.
Every prayer warrior who carried me and still do, Daphne whose continuous prayers I cannot do without. .
My family, and my Adams Clan especially Lindy for always being there for me. Apostle Peter John Smith, Apostle Rheede, Doctor Lynne Timms who also have loved ones above. My editor Grace, for doing an outstanding job.

PREFACE

The Bible says " Life and Death is in the Tongue of man and when one read through this book you cannot but see how the devil orchestrated deaths so that even we as Christians start to blame God for the devastation and heart ache that Satan brought on a man of God. It is so easy to speak out against God and asked Him as to why He allows the Devil to seek, steel, destroy and kill, if He is the God of love!

The purpose of this book is to expose the false ideology and analogy that God kills your loved ones and destroys your life as punishment for things that you have done during your life time. Don't be fooled, in siding with the voice that reminds you of your sins and past life, you stand to lose your rightful place in heaven. Jesus is the Creator and God of all. He is the King of kings and the Lord of Lords. He did not come to condemn and take sides, no He came to extend love and grace.

Satan is the one that destroy people's lives and kill to prevent us from accepting God and takes all measures to take you to hell with them. Jesu brought eternal life, immortality on the cross and is a fact that all people, saved and unsaved has to die some or other time, but the importance is that where you are going to spend your eternal life? Heaven or Hell. If you choose Jesus, then you will be with Him in the New Jerusalem. Denying Jesus Christ as God and conforming to the will of Satan will surely land you in Hell and even in the pool of Fire! Let's look at who the culprit of early death and destruction is!

Joh 10:10 The thief cometh not, but for to steal, and to kill, and to destroy: I am come that they might have life, and that they might have it more abundantly.

This book is surely one of the most compelling studies On Death and Grieve that grew out of Dr Raphael Sam Koopmans's tragic experience on death, life and transition. In this remarkable book, Dr Koopman explores the stages of death: denial and isolation, anger, bargaining, depression and acceptance.

Through various writing styles, he gives the reader a better understanding of how imminent death affects the person's family, and bringing hope to all who are involved in the tragedy of losing a loved one!

Professor Ed Van Den Bergh
Chancellor for Immanuel Christian University

DESCRIPTION

In dealing with painful loss, Doctor Koopman often fearfully and strongly ask real questions like, 'What am I going to do with my life? How will I get through each day? What if I never stop crying? Why did God let this happen?'

.

The journey of healing is a long one that requires time, patience and loving support. God understands our pain. He is there to give us the courage and strength to move forward. Turning to God as a source of wisdom can help us through such a difficult process.

One of the most compelling studies On Death and Grieve grew out of the tragic experience on death, life and transition I had. In this remarkable book, I explore the now-famous stages of death: denial and isolation, anger, bargaining, depression and acceptance. Through various writing styles, the reader a better gains understanding of how imminent death affects the person's family, then he directs us to the eternal hope that all of us have.

INTRODUCTION

Coping with losing a close friend or family member may be one of the hardest challenges which many of us face. When we lose a spouse, sibling, or parent, our grief can be particularly intense. Loss is understood as a natural part of life, but we can still be overcome by shock and confusion, leading to prolonged periods of sadness or depression. The sadness typically diminishes in intensity as time passes, but grieving is an important process to overcome these feelings so you can continue to embrace the time you had with your loved one.

Everyone reacts differently to death and employs personal coping mechanisms for grief. Research shows that most people can recover from loss on their own with time, if they have social support and healthy habits. It may take months or a year to come to terms with loss. There is no "normal" period for someone to grieve. Don't expect to pass through phases of grief either, as research suggests that most people do not go through these stages as progressive steps.

If your relationship with the deceased was difficult, this will also add another dimension to the grieving process. It may take some time and thought before you can look back on the relationship and adjust to the loss.

Human beings are naturally resilient, considering most of us can endure loss and then continue with our own lives. But some people may struggle with grief for longer periods and feel unable to carry out daily activities. Individuals with severe grief or complicated grief could benefit from the help of a psychologist or another licensed mental health professional with a specialization in grief.

Grief is a strong, sometimes overwhelming emotion for people, regardless of whether your sadness stems from the loss of a loved one or from a terminal diagnosis you or someone you love have received.

You might find yourself feeling numb and removed from daily life, unable to carry on with regular duties while saddled with your sense of loss. This feeling is still with me.

Grief is the natural reaction to loss. Grief is both a universal and a personal experience. Individual experiences of grief vary and are influenced by the nature of the loss. Some examples of loss include the death of a loved one, the ending of an important relationship, job loss, loss through theft, or the loss of independence through disability.

Midnight tears as a title reminds how most human beings are alone during midnight. Sometimes sleep escapes due to physical or emotional pain.
The pain often becomes so much that it drives us to tears. Midnight Tears is what I have whenever I miss my son. Tears which I'm the lonely hours of midnight flows from my being.. It is true that I can wipe the tears from my eyes but midnight returns periodically.

In my anguish, I was moved to pen my story. The story of a father who had a remarkable gift in a Son that was so precious that Heaven required Darian back.

Experts, if they exist; advise those grieving to realize that you can't controll the process and must prepare for varying stages of grief. Understanding why you're suffering can help, as can talking to others and trying to resolve issues that cause significant emotional pain, such as feeling guilty for a loved one's death.

Mourning can last for months or years. Generally, pain is tempered as time passes and as the bereaved adapts to life without a loved one, to the news of a terminal diagnosis, or to the realization that someone you love may die.

THE PLANNED TRIP

"A man's mind plans his way (as he journeys through life); But the Lord directs his steps amd establishes them" Proverbs 16:9 Amplified Bible.

My son Darian amd I were always close and grew closer over time sharing all monsters every detail of our lives. This also since my two sons lost their loving mother at a very young age. For months we were looking forward with excitement to quality time together exploring the Ceres valley of the Western Cape. Our plan was for us to be there for two weeks, Darian to wait until I wrap up the mission in the northern cape by December so we could start something new together back in the Western Cape.

The afternoon I board the bus I called Darian to confirm that his brother Lyle was going to join my 160 kilometers further.Darian shared how he bought himself a pair of new sneakers for walking in Ceres. Sneakers which is part of a collection I now treasure. My son spring cleaned his room, packed a bag and was readily waiting on me. Lyle and I were just hours away. While on the bus I video called my son, we had a nice chat and he was having dinner. I remember me saying, "I love you" with him repeating the same. These words were part of our weekly rhetoric.

I somehow later felt burdened and called Darian again. This time the phone was off, something which worried me. I tried his grandfather's number and there too was no response. I regret to this day not calling for help. A pain which cuts deep through me every time I think back of perhaps how things could have been better. Better for me ? Perhaps so.

Early upon arriving in Belville, I had a call from my sons Aunty Lasha who told me that something serious had happened. I was so afraid to ask details but in my mind I tough the unthinkable. They came to get me in belville and on our way I talked non stop about the resurrection amd the Almighty power of God. I already began praying whilst waiting on Lasha. I believed that God was able to bring my son back just as he did Lazarus.

Entering the room, seeing my son's body laying on the bed I still believed God would do this one thing for me I bargained with God, even reminding Him of the years of prayers in which I entrusted my children into Him. When what I pleaded for, did not happened, I began to blame God.

My outbursts, my cries, was seen by some as madness, religious people condemned me for the honest way I dealt with Abba. I remembered at the loss of my wife how the late Reverend Paul Manny who also lost his first wife young; told me this; "Sam" he said with his stern voice and ever so intelligent manner, "God is big enough to handle our questions. As His child, beat against Father's chest until you can no more. You will then find Him embracing you with His strong arms." I am still crying midnight Tears whilst beating on God's chest. This pain requires a real and close encounter with God Himself. An encounter no human can facilitate or make possible. I am coming to the Kingdom at whatever cost because only the balm of Gilead can heal my fractured soul.

The pain I am in, symbolically makes me weep blood tears. It is a pain so intense that I do not wish it on anyone else Only a Master Physician such as the Lord Jesus Christ can bring about the healing required. Something I, at this stage do not know even if it is possible. It feels like my soul is torn, my heart ripped out of my body. I can cry and keep crying but my son is not returning. The only consolation there is, is our reunion, something to which I long for and look forward to with eagerness.

I no longer ask, if there is a God. I now ask, where is He! Deep down I realize that He is real and therefore Heaven is real. This knowledge brings me to the secure position that my son is okay. He is fine. He is reunited with his Mommy, my late wife, whom he loves so much and they are in perfect Mansions. This was confirmed by a dear friend, Daphne in Ireland, as she was interceding she got this message amd shared with me.

As deep as the pain, so much real is the truth of a destiny that a loving God has prepared for His Masterpiece. We are a piece of the Master and one day all of us return to the Master Himself. None lost.

LOSS OF A LOVED ONE

The death of a child can take the form of a loss in infancy such as miscarriage or stillbirth or neonatal death, SIDS, or the death of an older child. Among adults over the age of 50, approximately 11% have been predeceased by at least one of their offspring.

Losing a loved one is one of the most distressing and, unfortunately, common experiences people face. Most people experiencing normal grief and bereavement have a period of sorrow, numbness, and even guilt and anger. Gradually these feelings ease, and it's possible to accept the loss and move forward.

For some people, feelings of loss are debilitating and don't improve even after time passes. This is known as complicated grief, sometimes called persistent complex bereavement disorder. In complicated grief, painful emotions are so long-lasting and severe that you have trouble recovering from the loss and resuming your own life.

Different people follow different paths through the grieving experience. The order and timing of these phases may vary from person to person:

- Accepting the reality of your loss
- Allowing yourself to experience the pain of your loss
- Adjusting to a new reality in which the deceased is no longer present
- Having other relationships

These differences are normal. But if you're unable to move through these stages more than a year after the death of a loved one, you may have complicated grief. If so, seek treatment. It can help you come to terms with your loss and reclaim a sense of acceptance and peace.

In most cases, parents like I do, find the grief almost unbearably devastating, and it tends to hold greater risk factors than any other loss. This loss also bears a lifelong process: one does not get 'over' the death but instead must assimilate and live with it. Intervention and comforting support can make all the difference to the survival of a parent in this type of grief but the risk factors are great and may include family breakup or suicide.

Feelings of guilt, whether legitimate or not, are pervasive, and the dependent nature of the relationship disposes parents to a variety of problems as they seek to cope with this great loss. Parents who suffer miscarriage or a regretful or coerced abortion may experience resentment towards others who experience successful pregnancies.

When I lost my wife at a young age with our marriage still in the honeymoon phase, our sons being only 11 months and our eldest 3 years old it was very painful. I just wanted to die too. I could not comprehend why God whom I have dedicated my entire life to since birth, could allow such tragedy and pain

.

I was left in a desert with no direction, no life experience with my two small boys. Like a boat, without a rudder, I drifted on the large ocean of life. I made many mistakes regrettably, the biggest and most painful; being not spending enough time with my sons. If only I could have a second chance, I definitely would have been more with my sons. This is a pain that I will carry to my grave.

Gracefully my sons Darian and Lyle grew up with Darian pursuing an LLB at the University of the western cape. Darian a born leader was serious and career-oriented. Lyle, on the other hand, was more playful with an almost carefree attitude Darian and I were both excited for his future and I registered at the same University when he started his lifter year as an LLB student.

We had great plans for a wonderful and bright life ahead. The year 2020 came and turned out to had been the worst for most people across the globe. The Covid19 pandemic not only tore families apart through death but economically people suffered everywhere.

The same year was my son Darian's semi-final year. We were both excited for him to graduate. He was going to apply at the University to lecture part-time whilst pursuing a medicine degree and fulfill his passion to help people by becoming a Doctor. I was also going to assist him to complete theological studies since he shared how God has called him to the ministry. My son, Darian was very passionate about helping others and would many times give his last to others without ever thinking about it again. He so reminded me of his Mother who as a norm would give her last to others. .

Since Darian lived with his grandfather closer to University, Lyle and I was traveling on a bus to him. Darian and I were going to go on a Field trip upon my arrival. Everything was arranged and we both could not wait to spend quality time together. While Lyle and I were on the bus journey of about ten hours overnight, I chat Darian up and even video call. He shared how he cleaned up, did his laundry, bought a pair of sneakers for hiking, and with his bag packed, he just waited upon me.

How indescribable the pain, how deep the longing still, when I remember my attempts to call my son while on the bus as well as early that morning and found his phone off. I sort of expected something negative when his aunts called me. My heart beated wildly with fear and panic. Lasha eventually fetched me at the bus stop and took me to Pa's house. I walked into the room to find my son's body on the bed. It was too late for our trip.

I had lost a few loved ones, as well as people close to me but this time it was different- the cut was close, part of my heart was torn away. So now and then the pain returns with the longing. Time is a temporary cover, but time does not heal.

As a minister I many a time encouraged those who had to bury their loved ones, however this time there was no encouragement for me. I had to press into God myself until I came to understand something so powerful about life that it shifted my mindset and my belief system.

I know now as a matter of fact that we live in a body, not the body living in us, and that this body has to remain on earth from where it was taken. Once this occurs the life goes back to its origin which is the Eternal Life, known to us as God. My understanding about him now is that life cannot be destroyed. It cannot die because it is alive. It just departs to another place where it continues. Life cannot die for Life is alive.

The Jewish Kabbalah teaches that God is Almighty Love. A Love that is compassionate, pur and unconditional. There is nothing we can do to deserve God's Love and nothing we can do to make God stop loving us. No matter what, no human can change God's view.

He loves us like a parent loves a child. Sometimes we may not agree with what the child does and we might even dislike our children's actions or behavior, however, we do not ever stop loving our children.

What do you call me now that I "lost" my son?
"Someone once said, 'when husbands lose wives they are called widowers and vice versa. Children losing parents are named orphans. And so the list continues. However, have you noticed that there is no name for a parent losing a child?" So I thought intently on this and this is my resolve. It is because our children are never lost. God is a Father and our children in His Presence are not lost, they are Home with our real Daddy. That includes all of us. Since we are all ABBA's children. We are all gonna be

WHAT IS GRIEF

Grief is a natural response to loss. It's the emotional suffering you feel when something or someone you love is taken away. I felt is so deeply and still feel it. Often, the pain of loss can feel overwhelming. You may experience all kinds of difficult and unexpected emotions, from shock or anger to disbelief, guilt, and profound sadness. The pain of grief can also disrupt your physical health, making it difficult to sleep, eat, or even think straight. These are normal reactions to loss—and the more significant the loss, the more intense your grief will be.

Mourning is an intimate and unique experience for each of us. There's no manual on how to cope with loss and certainly no right or wrong way to go through the stages of grief that might come from it.

Generally, when people hear the word grief, the death of a friend or loved one comes to mind. However, any loss that results in a significant change in a life circumstance or role can cause feelings of loss or grief. It is not uncommon to wonder why you feel overwhelmed or to question how long you will experience these feelings. If you are experiencing grief, it is okay to feel a shift in emotions or to even experience times that you feel emotionally unstable. It's important to allow yourself to grieve and to know when to seek help if grief becomes complicated or overwhelming to help prevent long-term mental health challenges.

It is important to understand that grief is not a single emotion; it's an experience or state of being that manifests itself physically, emotionally, mentally, and or spiritually following a painful or traumatic event. Moreover, like our fingerprints, each of us is unique and how we experience grief, and how long we grieve, can vary considerably from one person to another, even following similar loss situations, such as the death of a parent, spouse/partner, child, pet, etc.

That said, even though everyone experiences grief, there is a difference between normal, uncomplicated, or simple grief and abnormal, complicated, or exaggerated grief.
Grief is universal. At some point in everyone's life, there will be at least one encounter with grief. It may be from the death of a loved one, the loss of a job, the end of a relationship, or any other change that alters life as you know it.

Grief is also very personal. It's not very neat or linear. It doesn't follow any timelines or schedules. You may cry, become angry, withdraw, feel empty. None of these things are unusual or wrong. Everyone grieves differently, but there are some commonalities in the stages and the order of feelings experienced during grief.

The key to understanding grief is realizing that no one experiences the same thing. Grief is very personal, and you may feel something different every time. You may need several weeks, or grief may be years long.

If you decide you need help coping with the feelings and changes, a mental health professional is a good resource for vetting your feelings and finding a sense of assurance in these very heavy and weighty emotions.

Coping with the loss of someone or something you love is one of life's biggest challenges. You may associate grieving with the death of a loved one—which is often the cause of the most intense type of grief—but any loss can cause grief, including:

1. Divorce or relationship breakup
2. Loss of health
3. Losing a job
4. Loss of financial stability
5. A miscarriage
6. Retirement
7. Death of a pet
8. Loss of a cherished dream
9. A loved one's serious illness
10. Loss of a friendship
11. Loss of safety after a trauma
12. Selling the family home

Even subtle losses in life can trigger a sense of grief. For example, you might grieve after moving away from home, graduating from college, or changing jobs.

Whatever your loss, it's personal to you, so don't feel ashamed about how you feel, or believe that it's somehow only appropriate to grieve for certain things. This is exactly how I am feeling. If the person, animal, relationship, or situation was significant to you, it's normal to grieve the loss you're experiencing. Whatever the cause of your grief, though, there are healthy ways to cope with the pain that, in time, can ease your sadness and help you come to terms with your loss, find new meaning, and eventually move on with your life.However this is so tough, I honestly do not know when I will get here

People might notice or show grief in several ways:

• Physical reactions: These might be things like changes in appetite or sleep, an upset stomach, tight chest, crying, tense muscles, trouble relaxing, low energy, restlessness, or trouble concentrating.

• Frequent thoughts: These may be happy memories of the person who died, worries or regrets, or thoughts of what life will be like without the person.

• Strong emotions: For example, sadness, anger, guilt, despair, relief, love, or hope.

• Spiritual reactions: This might mean finding strength in faith, questioning religious beliefs, or discovering spiritual meaning and connections.

Grief is the perfectly natural, necessary, and normal way in which people respond to a personally painful or traumatic event. While everyone experiences grief in their way, most survivors normally exhibit some/all of the following characteristics temporarily when responding to a loss in the days, weeks, or months after the death of a loved one:

• Tears, crying or sobbing

• Sleep pattern changes, such as difficulty falling asleep or too little/too much sleep

• An overall lack of energy

• Feeling lethargic or apathetic about the day's necessary tasks or life in general

• Changes in appetite, such as not feeling like eating or consuming too much, particularly junk food

• Withdrawing from normal/usual social interactions and relationships

• Difficulty concentrating or focusing on a task, whether at work, personally, a hobby, etc.

• Questioning spiritual or religious beliefs, job/career choices, or life goals

• Feelings of anger, guilt, loneliness, depression, emptiness, sadness, etc. but still occasionally experiencing moments of joy/happiness

Everyone grieves a loss due to death in their unique way, and there is no timetable for grief. However, most grievers experience some/all of these reactions most profoundly in the immediate days/weeks following a loss but gradually return to a "new normal" in the weeks/months afterward. You won't entirely forget your loved ones as if they never existed, but in time, you will learn how to cope with their absence and the scar on your heart and soul.

When people have these reactions and emotions, we say they're grieving. I am grieving amd will still probably for a long time. Let’s look at the grieving process.

THE GRIEVING PROCESS

Grieving is a highly individual experience; and I agree that there’s no right or wrong way to grieve. How you grieve depends on many factors, including your personality and coping style, your life experience, your faith, and how significant the loss was to you. And even one’s faith goes through the fire.

Grief is a reaction to lose, but it's also the name we give to the process of coping with the loss of someone who has died. Grief is a healthy process of feeling comforted, coming to terms with a loss and finding ways to adapt.

Getting over grief doesn't mean forgetting about a person who has died. Healthy grief is about finding ways to remember loved ones and adjust to life without them present. This statement makes me open to the process of grieving since I will always remember my son. .

People often experience grief reactions in "waves" that come and go. Often, grief is most intense soon after someone has died. But some people don't feel their grief right away. They may feel numbness, shock, or disbelief. It can take time for the reality to sink in that the person is gone and merely temporarily.

Inevitably, the grieving process takes time. Healing happens gradually; it can’t be forced or hurried—and there is no “normal” timetable for grieving. Some people start to feel better in weeks or months. For others, the grieving process is measured in years. Whatever your grief experience, it’s important to be patient with yourself and allow the process to naturally unfold.

If someone you know has died, it's natural to keep having feelings and questions for a while even should such questions be offensive. . It's also natural to begin to feel a bit better. A lot depends on how a loss affects your life.

It's OK to feel grief for days, weeks, or even longer. How intensely you feel grief can be related to things like whether the loss was sudden or expected, or how close you felt to the person who died. Every person and situation is different.

Feeling better usually happens gradually. At times, it might feel like you'll never recover. The grieving process takes time, and grief can be more intense at some times than others.

As time goes on, reminders of the person who has died can intensify feelings of grief. At other times, it might feel as if grief is in the background of your normal activities, and not on your mind all the time.

As you do things you enjoy and spend time with people you feel good around, you can help yourself feel better. Grief has its own pace. Every situation is different. How much grief you feel or how long it lasts isn't a measure of how important the person was to you.

When you are grieving, it can feel like a very lonely time. It's important to know, however, that you are not alone. Everyone experiences grief from time to time in life. It is a normal reaction to loss. The best way to move forward after a loss is to allow yourself to go through the stages of grief.

Remember that you should not compare the way you grieve with how someone else is dealing with grief. Some people go through stages with little difficulty and find inner peace and the strength to move on with life without complications. Others may experience one or more stages more than once and for different lengths of time. Recognizing where you are in the process and knowing when to seek help can be helpful.

There's no "normal" amount of time to grieve. Your grieving process depends on several things, like your personality, age, beliefs, and support network. The type of loss is also a factor. For example, chances are you'll grieve longer and harder over the sudden death of a loved one than, say, the end of a romantic relationship.

Hopefully my sadness will ease with time, as study suggests.. It is said that a person will be able to feel happiness and joy along with grief. Many do return to daily life

MYTHS AND FACTS

Myth:
The pain will go away faster if you ignore it

Fact:
Trying to ignore your pain or keep it from surfacing will only make it worse in the long run. For real healing, it is necessary to face your grief and actively deal with it.

Myth:
It is important to "be strong" in the face of loss.

Fact:
Feeling sad, frightened, or lonely is a normal reaction to loss. Crying doesn't mean you are weak. You don't need to "protect" your family or friends by putting on a brave front. Showing your true feelings can help them and you

Myth:
If you don't cry, it means you aren't sorry about the loss.

Fact:
Crying is a normal response to sadness, but it's not the only one. Those who don't cry may feel the pain just as deeply as others. They may simply have other ways of showing it.

Myth:
Grieving should last about a year.

Fact:
There is no specific time frame for grieving. How long it takes differs from person to person.

Myth:
Moving on with your life means forgetting about your loss.

Fact:
Moving on means you've accepted your loss—but that's not the same as forgetting. You can move on with your life and keep the memory of someone or something you lost as an important part of yourself. As we move through life, these memories can become more and more integral to defining the people we are.

DEALING WITH GRIEVE

While grieving and loss is an inevitable part of life, there are ways to help cope with the pain, come to terms with your grief, and eventually, find a way to pick up the pieces and move on with your life. Something I cannot imagine right now.

It is important to remember that everyone copes with loss differently. While you may find that you experience all five stages of grief, you may also find that it is difficult to classify your feelings into any one of the stages. Have patience with yourself and your feelings in dealing with loss.

Take a moment to notice how you've been feeling and reacting. Try to put it into words. Write about what you're feeling and the ways you're reacting to grief. Notice how it feels to think about and write about your experience

.

Think of someone you can share your feelings with, someone who will listen and understand. Find time to talk to that person about what you're going through and how the loss is affecting you. Notice how you feel after sharing and talking.

We can learn a lot from the people in our lives. Even when you don't feel like talking, it can help just to be with others who also loved the person who died. When family and friends get together, it helps people feel less isolated in the first days and weeks of their grief. Being with others helps you, and your presence — and words — can support them, too.

Allow yourself time to process all of your emotions, and when you are ready to speak about your experiences with loved ones or a healthcare professional, do so. If you are supporting someone who has lost a loved one, remember that you don't need to do anything specific, but allow them room to talk about it when they are ready.

□ Acknowledge your pain.
□ Accept that grief can trigger many different and unexpected emotions. □ Understand that your grieving process will be unique to you.
□ Seek out face-to-face support from people who care about you.
□ Support yourself emotionally by taking care of yourself physically.
□ Recognize the difference between grief and depression.

STAGES OF GRIEVE

Your feelings may happen in phases as you come to terms with your loss. You can't control the process, but it's helpful to know the reasons behind your feelings. All people experience grief differently.

Exploring the stages of grief and loss could help you understand and put into context where you are in your grieving process and what you feel.

Similarly, if you're concerned or want to understand someone else's grieving process, remember that there's no one way of going through it. Everyone mourns differently. You could go through many intense emotions, or you could seemingly not react at all. Both responses are valid and not uncommon.

How much time you spend navigating the stages of grief also varies from person to person. It might take you hours, months, or longer to process a loss and heal from it.
You might not experience all these stages of grief or in the order listed above. You could go back and forth from one stage to another.

You may even skip all these emotions and process your loss differently altogether. The stages of grief are supposed to serve you as a reference, not as a rule. Though it is no longer considered the ideal way to think about grief, you may have heard of the stages of grief:

- **Denial**

  The first stage in this theory, denial helps us minimize the overwhelming pain of loss. As we process the reality of our loss, we are also trying to survive emotional pain. It can be hard to believe we have lost an important person in our lives, especially when we may have just spoken with this person the previous week or even the previous day.

  Our reality has shifted completely in this moment of loss. It can take our minds some time to adjust to this new reality. We are reflecting on the experiences we have shared with the person we lost and we might find ourselves wondering how to move forward in life without this person.

  This is a lot of information to explore and a lot of painful imagery to process. Denial attempts to slow this process down and take us through it one step at a time, rather than risk the potential of feeling overwhelmed by our emotions.

  Denial is not only an attempt to pretend that the loss does not exist. We are also trying to absorb and understand what is happening.
  When you first learn of a loss, it's normal to think, "This isn't happening." You may feel shocked or numb. This is a temporary way to deal with the rush of overwhelming emotion. It's a defense mechanism. For some people, this may be the first response to loss.

Denial is a common defense mechanism. It may help you buffer the immediate shock of the hurtful situation.
As an immediate reaction, you might doubt the reality of the loss at first.

A few examples of this type of denial are:

- If you're facing the death of a loved one, you might find yourself fantasizing someone will call to say there's been a mistake and nothing happened.

- If you're dealing with a breakup, you might convince yourself your partner will soon regret leaving and come back to you.

- If you lost your job, you might feel your former boss will offer you the position back after they realize they've made a mistake.

Grief is an overwhelming emotion. It's not unusual to respond to the intense and often sudden feelings by pretending the loss or change isn't happening. Denying it gives you time to more gradually absorb the news and begin to process it. This is a common defense mechanism and helps numb you to the intensity of the situation.

As you move out of the denial stage, however, the emotions you've been hiding will begin to rise. You'll be confronted with a lot of sorrow you've denied. That is also part of the journey of grief, but it can be difficult.

It's common in this stage to wonder how life will go on in this different state – you are in a state of shock because life as you once knew it, has changed in an instant. If you were diagnosed with a deadly disease, you might believe the news is incorrect – a mistake must have occurred somewhere in the lab–they mixed up your blood work with someone else. If you receive news on the death of a loved one, perhaps you cling to a false hope that they identified the wrong person. In the denial stage, you are not living in 'actual reality,' rather, you are living in a 'preferable' reality. Interestingly, it is denial and shock that help you cope and survive the grief event. Denial aids in pacing your feelings of grief. Instead of becoming completely overwhelmed with grief, we deny it, do not accept it, and stagger its full impact on us at one time. Think of it as your body's natural defense mechanism saying "hey, there's only so much I can handle at once." Once the denial and shock started to fade, the start of the healing process begins. At this point, those feelings that you were once suppressing are coming to the surface.

After this first reaction of shock and denial, you may go numb for a while.

At some point, you could feel like nothing matters to you anymore. Life as you once knew it has changed. It might be difficult to feel you can move on.

This is a natural reaction that helps you process the loss in your own time. By going numb, you're giving yourself time to explore at your own pace the changes you're going through.

Denial is a temporary response that carries you through the first wave of pain. Eventually, when you're ready, the feelings and emotions you have denied will resurface, and your healing journey will continue.

- **Anger**

Sometimes pain takes other forms. According to Kübler-Ross, pain from a loss is often redirected and expressed as anger.

Feeling intensely angry might surprise you or your loved ones, but it's not uncommon. This anger serves a purpose. It might be particularly overwhelming for some people to feel anger because, in many cultures, anger is a feared or rejected emotion. You might be more used to avoiding it than confronting it.

During the anger stage of grief, you might start asking questions like "Why me?" or "What did I do to deserve this?"

You could also feel suddenly angry at inanimate objects, strangers, friends, or family members. You might feel angry at life itself.

Where denial may be considered a coping mechanism, anger is a masking effect. Anger is hiding many of the emotions and pain that you carry. This anger may be redirected at other people, such as the person who died, your ex, or your old boss. You may even aim your anger at inanimate objects.

Once you start to live in 'actual' reality again and not in 'preferable' reality, anger might start to set in. This is a common stage to think "why me?" and "life's not fair!"

You might look to blame others for the cause of your grief and also may redirect your anger to close friends and family. You find it incomprehensible how something like this could happen to you. If you are strong in faith, you might start to question your belief in God. "Where is God? Why didn't he protect me?" Researchers and mental health professionals agree that this anger is a necessary stage of grief. And encourage anger. It's important to truly feel the anger. It's thought that even though you might seem like you are in an endless cycle of anger, it will dissipate – and the more you truly feel the anger, the more quickly it will dissipate, and the more quickly you will heal. It is not healthy to suppress your feelings of anger – it is a natural response – and perhaps, arguably, a necessary one. In everyday life, we are normally told to control our anger toward situations and others. When you experience a grief event, you might feel disconnected from reality – that you have no grounding anymore. Your life has shattered and there's nothing solid to hold onto. Think of anger as a strength to bind you to reality. You might feel deserted or abandoned during a grief event. That no one is there. You are alone in this world. The direction of anger toward something or somebody is what might bridge you back to reality and connect you to people again. It is a "thing." It's something to grasp onto – a natural step in healing.

While your rational brain knows the object of your anger isn't to blame, your feelings at that moment are too intense to feel that.

As reality sets in, you're faced with the pain of your loss. You may feel frustrated and helpless. These feelings later turn into anger. You might direct it toward other people, a higher power, or life in general. To be angry with a loved one who died and left you alone is natural, too.

It is common to experience anger after the loss of a loved one. We are trying to adjust to a new reality and we are likely experiencing extreme emotional discomfort. There is so much to process that anger may feel like it allows us an emotional outlet.

Keep in mind that anger does not require us to be very vulnerable. However, it tends to be more socially acceptable than admitting we are scared. Anger allows us to express emotion with less fear of judgment or rejection. Unfortunately, anger tends to be the first thing we feel when we start to release emotions related to lose. This can leave you feeling isolated in your experience and perceived as unapproachable by others in moments when we could benefit from comfort, connection, and reassurance.

Anger may mask itself in feelings like bitterness or resentment. It may not be clear-cut fury or rage. Not everyone will experience this stage, and some may linger here. As the anger subsides, however, you may begin to think more rationally about what's happening and feel the emotions you've been pushing aside.

Examples of the anger stage

- Breakup or divorce: "I hate him! He'll regret leaving me!"

- Job loss: "They're terrible bosses. I hope they fail."

- Death of a loved one: "If she cared for herself more, this wouldn't have happened."

- Terminal illness diagnosis: "Where is God in this? How dare God to let this happen

It's not rare to also feel anger toward the situation or person you lost. Rationally, you might understand the person isn't to blame. Emotionally, however, you may resent them for causing you pain or for leaving you.

At some point, you might also feel guilty for being angry. This could make you angrier.

Try reminding yourself that underneath your anger is pain. And even if it might not feel like it, this anger is necessary for healing.

Anger might also be a way to reconnect to the world after isolating yourself from it during the denial stage. When you're numb, you disconnect from everyone. When you're angry, you connect, even if through this emotion.

But anger isn't the only emotion you might experience during this stage. Irritability, bitterness, anxiety, rage, and impatience are just some other ways you might cope with your loss. It's all part of the same process.

- **Bargaining**

When coping with loss, it isn't unusual to feel so desperate that you are willing to do almost anything to alleviate or minimize the pain. Losing a loved one can cause us to consider any way we can avoid the current pain or the pain we are anticipating from loss. There are many ways we may try to bargain.

I remember my bargaining with God at losing my wife, and my son.

Bargaining can come in a variety of promises including:
o "God, if you can heal this person I will turn my life around."

o "I promise to be better if you will let this person live."
o "I'll never get angry again if you can stop him/her from dying or leaving me."

When bargaining starts to take place, we are often directing our requests to a higher power, or something bigger than we are that may be able to influence a different outcome.

There is an acute awareness of our humanness in these moments when we realize there is nothing we can do to influence change or a better result.

Bargaining is a way to hold on to hope in a situation of intense pain.

You might think to yourself that you're willing to do anything and sacrifice everything if your life is restored to how it was before the loss.

During this internal negotiation, you could find yourself thinking in terms of "what if" or "if only": what if I did XYZ, then everything will go back to normal; if only I had done something differently to prevent the loss.

Guilt might be an accompanying emotion during this stage as you inadvertently might be trying to regain some control, even if at your own expense.

All these emotions and thoughts aren't uncommon. As hard as it might feel, this helps you heal as you confront the reality of your loss.

During this stage, you dwell on what you could've done to prevent the loss. Common thoughts are "If only..." and "What if..." You may also try to strike a deal with a higher power.

In a way, this stage is false hope. You might falsely make yourself believe that you can avoid grief through a type of negotiation. If you change this, I'll change that. You are so desperate to get your life back to how it was before the grief event, you are willing to make a major life change in an attempt toward normality. Guilt is a common wingman of bargaining. This is when you endure the endless "what if" statements. What if I had left the house 5 minutes sooner – the accident would have never happened. What if I encouraged him to go to the doctor six months ago like I first thought – cancer could have been found sooner and he could have been saved.

This feeling of helplessness can cause us to react in protest by bargaining, which gives us a perceived sense of control over something that feels so out of control. While bargaining we also tend to focus on our faults or regrets.

We might look back at our interactions with the person we are losing and note all of the times we felt disconnected or may have caused them pain.

During grief, you may feel vulnerable and helpless. In those moments of intense emotions, it's not uncommon to look for ways to regain control or to want to feel like you can affect the outcome of an event. In the bargaining stage of grief, you may find yourself creating a lot of "what if" and "if only" statements.

It's also not uncommon for religious individuals to try to make a deal or promise to God or a higher power in return for healing or relief from the grief and pain. Bargaining is a line of defense against the emotions of grief. It helps you postpone the sadness, confusion, or hurt.

Examples of the bargaining stage:

• Breakup or divorce: "If only I had spent more time with her, she would have stayed."

• Job loss: "If only I worked more weekends, they would have seen how valuable I am."

• Death of a loved one: "If only I had called her that night, she wouldn't be gone."

• Terminal illness diagnosis: "If only we had gone to the doctor sooner, we could have stopped this."

It is common to recall times when we may have said things we did not mean, and wish we could go back and behave differently. We also tend to make the drastic assumption that if things had played out differently, we would not be in such an emotionally painful place in our lives.

- **Depression**

Depression is a commonly accepted form of grief. Most people associate depression immediately with grief – as it is a "present" emotion. It represents the emptiness we feel when we are living in reality and realize the person or situation is gone or over. In this stage, you might withdraw from life, feel numb, live in a fog, and not want to get out of bed. The world might seem too much and too overwhelming for you to face. You don't want to be around others, don't feel like talking, and experience feelings of hopelessness. You might even experience suicidal thoughts – thinking "what's the point of going on?"

Whereas anger and bargaining can feel very "active," depression may feel like a "quiet" stage of grief.
In the early stages of loss, you may be running from the emotions, trying to stay a step ahead of them. By this point, however, you may be able to embrace and work through them more healthfully. You may also choose to isolate yourself from others to fully cope with the loss.

During our experience of processing grief, there comes a time when our imaginations calm down and we slowly start to look at the reality of our present situation. Bargaining no longer feels like an option and we are faced with what is happening.

We start to feel the loss of our loved ones more abundantly. As our panic begins to subside, the emotional fog begins to clear and the loss feels more present and unavoidable. In those moments, we tend to pull inward as the sadness grows. We might find ourselves retreating, being less sociable, and reaching out less to others about what we are going through. Although this is a very natural stage of grief, dealing with depression after the loss of a loved one can be extremely isolating.

Sadness sets in as you begin to understand the loss and its effect on your life. Signs of depression include crying, sleep issues, and a decreased appetite. You may feel overwhelmed, regretful, and lonely.

That doesn't mean, however, that depression is easy or well defined. Like the other stages of grief, depression can be difficult and messy. It can feel overwhelming. You may feel foggy, heavy, and confused.

Depression may feel like the inevitable landing point of any loss. However, if you feel stuck here or can't seem to move past this stage of grief, talk with a mental health expert. A therapist can help you work through this period of coping.

- **Examples of the depression stage**

• Breakup or divorce: “Why go on at all?”

• Job loss: “I don’t know how to go forward from here.”

• Death of a loved one: “What am I without her / him?”

• Terminal illness diagnosis: “My whole life comes to this terrible end.”

Just as in all the other stages of grief, depression is experienced in different ways. There’s no right or wrong way to go about it, nor is there a deadline to overcome it.

- **Acceptance**

The last stage of grief is acceptance. Not in the sense that “it’s okay my husband died” rather, “my husband died, but I’m going to be okay.” In this stage, your emotions may begin to stabilize. You re-enter reality. You come to terms with the fact that the “new” reality is that your partner is never coming back – or that you are going to succumb to your illness and die soon – and you’re okay with that. It’s not a “good” thing – but it’s something you can live with.

It is a time of adjustment and readjustment. There are good days, there are bad days, and then there are good days again. In this stage, it does not mean you’ll never have another bad day – where you are uncontrollably sad. But, the good days tend to outnumber the bad days. In this stage, you may lift from your fog, you start to engage with friends again, and might even make new relationships as time goes on. You understand your loved one can never be replaced, but you move, grow, and evolve into your new reality.

In this final stage of grief, you accept the reality of your loss. It can't be changed. Although you still feel sad, you're able to start moving forward with your life.

When we come to a place of acceptance, it is not that we no longer feel the pain of loss. However, we are no longer resisting the reality of our situation, and we are not struggling to make it something different.

Sadness and regret can still be present in this phase, but the emotional survival tactics of denial, bargaining, and anger are less likely to be present.

Reaching acceptance isn't necessarily about being OK with what happened. Depending on your experience, it might be understandable if you don't ever feel this way.

Acceptance is more about how you acknowledge the losses you've experienced, how you learn to live with them, and how you readjust your life accordingly.

You might feel more comfortable reaching out to friends and family during this stage, but it's also natural to feel you prefer to withdraw at times.

You may also feel like you accept the loss at times and then move to another stage of grief again. This back-and-forth between stages is natural and a part of the healing process. In time, you may eventually find yourself stationed at this stage for long periods.

That doesn't mean you'll never feel sadness or anger again toward your loss, but your long-term perspective about it and how you live with this reality will be different.

Acceptance is not necessarily a happy or uplifting stage of grief. It doesn't mean you've moved past the grief or loss. It does, however, mean that you've accepted it and have come to understand what it means in your life now.

You may feel very different in this stage. That's entirely expected. You've had a major change in your life, and that upends the way you feel about many things. Look to acceptance as a way to see that there may be more good days than bad, but there may still be bad — and that's OK.

Examples of the acceptance stage:

• Breakup or divorce: "Ultimately, this was a healthy choice for me.

• Job loss: "I'll be able to find a way forward from here and can start a new path."

• Death of a loved one: "I am so fortunate to have had so many wonderful years with him, and he will always be in my memories."

• Terminal illness diagnosis: "I have the opportunity to tie things up and make sure I get to do what I want in these final weeks and months."

If you are experiencing any of these emotions following a loss, it may help to know that your reaction is natural and that you'll heal in time. However, not everyone who grieves goes through all of these stages—and that's okay

Contrary to popular belief, you do not have to go through each stage to heal. Some people resolve their grief without going through any of these stages. And if you do go through these stages of grief, you probably won't experience them in neat, sequential order, so don't worry about what you "should" be feeling or which stage you're supposed to be in.

"They were never meant to help tuck messy emotions into neat packages. They are responses to lose that many people have, but there is not a typical response to loss, as there is no typical loss. Our grieving is as individual as our lives."

GRIEF VS DEPRESSION:

Distinguishing between grief and clinical depression isn't always easy as they share many symptoms, but there are ways to tell the difference. Remember, grief can be a roller coaster. It involves a wide variety of emotions and a mix of good and bad days. Even when you're in the middle of the grieving process, you will still have moments of pleasure or happiness. With depression, on the other hand, the feelings of emptiness and despair are constant.

Where grief and depression differ is that grief tends to decrease over time and occurs in waves that are triggered by thoughts or reminders of its cause. In other words, the person may feel relatively better while in certain situations, such as when friends and family are around to support them. But triggers like the birthday of a deceased loved one or going to a wedding after having finalized a divorce could cause the feelings to resurface more strongly.

Depression, on the other hand, tends to be more persistent and pervasive. An exception to this would be atypical depression, in which positive events can bring about an improvement in mood. A person with atypical depression, however, tends to exhibit symptoms that are the opposite of those commonly experienced with grief, such as sleeping excessively, eating more, and gaining weight.

Other symptoms that suggest depression, not just grief, include:

- Intense, pervasive sense of guilt
- Thoughts of suicide or a preoccupation with dying
- Feelings of hopelessness or worthlessness
- Slow speech and body movements

- Inability to function at home, work, and/or school
- Seeing or hearing things that aren't there

Everyone grieves differently. Some people may have symptoms that are very similar to depression, such as withdrawal from social settings and intense feelings of sadness. However, there are very important differences between depression and grief.

Symptom duration: People with depression feel depressed almost all the time. Grieving people often have symptoms that fluctuate or come in waves.

Acceptance of support: People with depression often begin to isolate themselves and may even shun others. People who are grieving may avoid vibrant social settings, but they often accept some support from loved ones.

Ability to function: Someone who is grieving may still be able to go to work or school. They may even feel that participating in these activities will help occupy their mind. However, if you're clinically depressed, you may experience symptoms so severe that you're unable to go to work or do other important tasks.

Grief can be a trigger for depression, but not everyone who grieves will experience depression.

Grief	Depression
There is an identifiable loss	A specific loss may or may
The person's focus is on the loss	The person's focus is on self
Fluctuating ability to feel pleasure	Inability to feel pleasure
Fluctuating physical symptoms	Prolonged and marked funct
Closeness of others is usually comforting	Persistent isolation from oth
Able to feel a wide range of emotions	Fixed emotions and feeling
May express guilt over some aspects of the loss	Has generalized feelings of
Self-esteem is usually preserved after the loss	Feelings of worthlessness an
Thoughts of death are typically related to wanting to be reunited with the deceased loved one	Thoughts of death related to undeserving of life or unable

SYMPTOMS OF GRIEF

While loss affects people in different ways, many of us experience the following symptoms when we're grieving. Just remember that almost anything that you experience in the early stages of grief is normal—including feeling like you're going crazy, feeling like you're in a bad dream, or questioning your religious or spiritual beliefs.

Emotional symptoms of grief

Shock and disbelief: Right after a loss, it can be hard to accept what happened. You may feel numb, have trouble believing that the loss really happened, or even deny the truth. If someone you love has died, you may keep expecting them to show up, even though you know they're gone.

Sadness: Profound sadness is probably the most universally experienced symptom of grief. You may have feelings of emptiness, despair, yearning, or deep loneliness. You may also cry a lot or feel emotionally unstable.

Guilt: You may regret or feel guilty about things you did or didn't say or do. You may also feel guilty about certain feelings (e.g. feeling relieved when the person died after a long, difficult illness). After a death, you may even feel guilty for not doing something to prevent the death, even if there was nothing more you could have done.

Anger: Even if the loss was nobody's fault, you may feel angry and resentful. If you lost a loved one, you may be angry with yourself, God, the doctors, or even the person who died for abandoning you. You may feel the need to blame someone for the injustice that was done to you.

Fear: A significant loss can trigger a host of worries and fears. You may feel anxious, helpless, or insecure. You may even have panic attacks. The death of a loved one can trigger fears about your mortality, of facing life without that person, or the responsibilities you now face alone.

Physical symptoms of grief

We often think of grief as a strictly emotional process, but grief often involves physical problems, including:

• Crying
• Headaches
• Difficulty Sleeping
• Questioning the Purpose of Life
• Questioning Your Spiritual Beliefs (e.g., your belief in God)
• Feelings of Detachment
• Isolation from Friends and Family
• Abnormal Behavior
• Worry
• Anxiety
• Frustration
• Guilt
• Fatigue
• Anger
• Loss of Appetite
• Aches, Pains, Stress

HELPING SOMEONE WHO GRIEVES

You've taken the first step by just wondering how you can help your loved one.

Here are some ways you can support them now and in the future.

1. Listen

Perhaps one of the main legacies from Elisabeth Kübler-Ross and her work is the importance of listening to the grieving person.

You might have the best intentions and want to provide comforting words. But in some instances, the best support comes from just being there and making it clear that you're available to listen to whatever — and whenever — they want to share.

It's also important to accept it if your loved one doesn't want to talk with you. Give them time and space.

2. Reach out

Not everyone knows how to to comfort others. It might be intimidating or overwhelming seeing someone you care about have a rough time.

But don't let these fears stop you from offering help or from being there. Lead with empathy, and the rest will follow.

3. Be practical

Look for ways to ease the weight off your loved one's shoulders. Explore the areas they might need help managing while they process their loss.

This could mean helping with food preparation or grocery shopping, organizing their room or house, or picking up their children from school.

4. Don't assume

You might want to verbally offer your support and be attentive to whatever they tell you might help them feel better. But avoid assuming or guessing "which step" of the process they're going through at the moment.

A smiley face or no tears don't necessarily mean they're not grieving. A change in their physical appearance doesn't mean they're depressed.

Wait for them to express how they feel, if they're ready, and go from there.

5. Search for resources

You might have the clarity of mind and the energy to browse local support groups and organizations, call an insurance company, and find a mental health professional.

The decision of reaching out for this kind of help is, of course, entirely up to the grieving person. But having the information at hand might save time whenever they're prepared or willing to take it.

COMMON MISCONCEPTIONS ABOUT GRIEVING

Because everyone mourns differently and for different reasons, sometimes you might feel your grieving process isn't going "according to the norm."

But remember, there's no such thing as a right or wrong way of coping with a loss.

These might be some of the thoughts that could cross your mind when looking at your own or someone else's way of grieving.

1. 'I am doing it wrong'

One of the most common misconceptions about grieving is that everyone goes through it in the same way.

When it comes to healing from a loss, there's no correct way of doing it. You might find it useful to remind yourself there's no "I should be feeling this way."

Grieving isn't about going over or following a setlist of steps. It's a unique and multidimensional healing journey.

2. 'I should be feeling…'

Not everyone experiences all the above-mentioned stages or even goes through these emotions the same way.

For example, maybe the depression stage feels more like irritability than sadness for you. And denial could be more of a sense of shock and disbelief than an actual expectation that something out of the blue will fix the loss.

The emotions used to contextualize the stages of grief aren't the only ones you'll experience. You might not even experience them at all, and that's natural too.

This is no indication that your healing journey is faulty in some way. Your healing experience is unique to you and valid nonetheless.

3. 'This goes first'

Remember, there's no specific or linear order for the stages of grief.

You could move along the stages one by one, or you could go back and forth. Some days you might feel very sad, and the very next day you could wake up feeling hopeful. Then you could go back to feeling sad. Some days you might even feel both!

In the same way, denial isn't necessarily the first emotion you'll experience. Maybe your first emotional reaction is anger or depression.

This is natural and part of the healing process.

4. 'It's taking too long

Coping with a loss is ultimately a deeply personal and singular experience. Many factors affect how long it takes.

Some people navigate through grief in a few days. Others take months or longer to process their loss.

You might find it useful to not set any deadlines for your process.

In grief, you'll experience some of these emotions in waves of intensity. In time, you'll notice this intensity decrease.

If you feel your emotions stay or increase in intensity and frequency, this might be a good time to seek professional support.

5. 'I'm depressed'

Going through the stages of grief, particularly the depression stage isn't equivalent to clinical depression. There's a distinction between having clinical depression and grieving.

This means that even though some symptoms might be similar, there are still key differences between both.

For example, in grief, the intense sadness will lessen in intensity and frequency as time goes by. You might even experience this sadness at the same time you find temporary relief in happy memories from times before the loss.

In clinical depression, on the other hand, without the proper treatment, your mood would stay negative or worsen with time. It would likely affect your self-esteem. You may rarely experience feelings of pleasure or happiness.

This doesn't mean there isn't a possibility you could develop clinical depression during the grieving process. If your emotions progressively increase in intensity and frequency, reach out for support.

Take care of yourself as you grieve

When you're grieving, it's more important than ever to take care of yourself. The stress of a major loss can quickly deplete your energy and emotional reserves. Looking after your physical and emotional needs will help you get through this difficult time.

Face your feelings.

You can try to suppress your grief, but you can't avoid it forever. To heal, you have to acknowledge the pain.

Trying to avoid feelings of sadness and loss only prolongs the grieving process. Unresolved grief can also lead to complications such as depression, anxiety, substance abuse, and health problems.

Express your feelings tangibly or creatively.

Write about your loss in a journal. If you've lost a loved one, write a letter saying the things you never got to say; make a scrapbook or photo album celebrating the person's life, or get involved in a cause or organization that was important to your loved one.

Try to maintain your hobbies and interests.

There's comfort in routine and getting back to the activities that bring you joy and connect you closer to others can help you come to terms with your loss and aid the grieving process.

Don't let anyone tell you how to feel, and don't tell yourself how to feel either. Your grief is your own, and no one else can tell you when it's time to "move on" or "get over it." Let yourself feel whatever you feel without embarrassment or judgment. It's okay to be angry, to yell at the heavens, to cry, or not to cry. It's also okay to laugh, to find moments of joy, and to let go when you're ready.

Plan ahead for grief "triggers."

Anniversaries, holidays, and milestones can reawaken memories and feelings. Be prepared for an emotional wallop, and know that it's completely normal. If you're sharing a holiday or lifecycle event with other relatives, talk to them ahead of time about their expectations and agree on strategies to honor the person you loved.

Look after your physical health.

The mind and body are connected. When you feel healthy physically, you'll be better able to cope emotionally. Combat stress and fatigue by getting enough sleep, eating right, and exercising. Don't use alcohol or drugs to numb the pain of grief or lift your mood artificially.

COMPLICATED GRIEF

Complicated grieve has many different descriptions. The most common one is that its acute grief that causes long periods of suffering after losing a loved one. Many doctors believe that it's related to adjustment disorder, which is when you show a long and intense response to a stressor.

Many doctors are now discovering that complicated grieve has many features of a disorder. Doctors once avoided giving treatment to people who were grieving. Grief has long been considered a personal, non-medical struggle. However, new evidence shows that complicated grieve can make you feel worthless and suicidal, which is similar to depression. Because of this, doctors now seek to treat complicated grief as a disorder, suggesting therapies and treatments to lessen the draining hurt of grief.

No exact number exists for how many people have or have had complicated grieve. One estimate states that 10 million people in the United States likely have severe enough symptoms to be thought of as having complicated grieve.

"Normal" grief in response to the death of a loved one generally affects mourners temporarily, and the majority of survivors gradually feel the characteristics of grief dissipate over time and can begin resuming their natural routines and activities. Some people, however, might experience complicated grief in which the usual responses to the death of a loved one do not fade over time and can impair or prevent them from leading their normal lives.

Complicated grief might be referred to by other terms, such as:

- Abnormal grief
- Chronic grief
- Complicated grief disorder
- Exaggerated grief
- Pathological grief
- Persistent complex bereavement disorder

Regardless of the terminology, the characteristics of complicated grief can include

- Anger, irritation, or episodes of rage
- An inability to focus on anything but the death of a loved one
- Focusing intensely on reminders of the deceased or excessive avoidance of such reminders
- Intense feelings of sadness, pain, detachment, sorrow, hopelessness, emptiness, low self-esteem, bitterness, or longing for the deceased's presence
- Problems accepting the reality of the death
- Self-destructive behavior, such as alcohol or drug abuse
- Suicidal thoughts or actions

As mentioned earlier, everyone's grief response is unique and there is no specific amount of time that defines when normal grief becomes complicated grief. Some impose a threshold of around six months after the death occurred,3 but it is perfectly normal for grievers to find the first year following a significant loss difficult as survivors experience holidays, birthdays, anniversaries, and other significant annual dates/events for the first time without their loved ones.

If you exhibit some of the characteristics of complicated grief above, still feel "trapped" in your grief, and/or that your grief response remains the same or has intensified despite the passage of several months or more, then you might consider seeking help from a mental health professional.

You should also consider joining a bereavement support group in your area, particularly if one exists for people who have experienced a similar type of loss (a spouse, partner, child, etc.) Grief typically causes feelings of isolation but discussing your situation with others mourning a death might help you gain a different perspective on your specific response.

SYMPTOMS OF COMPLICATED GRIEF

During the first few months after a loss, many signs and symptoms of normal grief are the same as those of complicated grief. However, while normal grief symptoms gradually start to fade over time, those of complicated grief linger or get worse. Complicated grief is like being in an ongoing, heightened state of mourning that keeps you from healing.

Signs and symptoms of complicated grief may include:

- Intense sorrow, pain, and rumination over the loss of your loved one
- Focus on little else but your loved one's death
- Extreme focus on reminders of the loved one or excessive avoidance of reminders
- Intense and persistent longing or pining for the deceased
- Problems accepting the death
- Numbness or detachment
- Bitterness about your loss
- Feeling that life holds no meaning or purpose
- Lack of trust in others
- Inability to enjoy life or think back on positive experiences with your loved one

Complicated grief also may be indicated if you continue to:

- Have trouble carrying out normal routines
- Isolate from others and withdraw from social activities
- Experience depression, deep sadness, guilt or self-blame
- Believe that you did something wrong or could have prevented the death
- Feel life isn't worth living without your loved one
- Wish you had died along with your loved one

At times, people with complicated grief may consider suicide. If you're thinking about suicide, talk to someone you trust.

Grieving is a normal process. However, it can worsen your quality of life and involve more serious symptoms when it lasts for a long time. These symptoms can include:

- a powerful pain when you think of your lost loved one
- a heightened focus on reminders of your lost loved one
- an overall feeling of numbness
- a feeling of bitterness when you think about your loss
- a loss of purpose or motivation
- a loss of trust in friends, family, and acquaintances
- an inability to enjoy life

If you have these symptoms for months or years, you may need to ask your doctor about treatment for complicated grief.

Symptoms of depression can be similar to complicated grief. If you've been diagnosed with depression, CG can make your symptoms worse. In addition to the complicated grief symptoms listed above, depression can cause other unique symptoms, such as:

- constant sadness, anxiety, or feelings of emptiness
- feelings of guilt or helplessness
- loss of interest in hobbies
- insomnia or oversleeping
- physical aches that don't go away with treatment
- suicidal thoughts or suicide attempts

You can have symptoms of both complicated grief and depression at the same time. However, complicated grief and depression must be treated differently.

Factors That Might/Might Not Contribute to Complicated Grief

Finally, depending upon the circumstances surrounding the death and/or the unique personalities/relationships of the people involved, certain challenges can occur that might—or might not—either contribute to complicated grief or make you wonder if you're experiencing complicated grief.

Delayed grief involves the postponement of a normal grief response until a later time, whether intentional or unconsciously. In some cases, an individual might need to "be strong" outwardly to help another loved one cope following a death, whether during the funeral arrangement process, service or interment, or in the weeks/months that follow. In other instances, someone might not begin grieving right after a death occurs because he or she already has too much stress, needs more time to process the reality of the loss, can't grieve until encountering a "grief trigger," etc.

Disenfranchised grief can occur when a grieving person feels he or she cannot openly acknowledge a loss to death because of real or imagined pressures exerted by his or her family/friends, cultural or religious beliefs, or society in general. Causes might include, for example, death related to HIV/AIDS, miscarriage or stillbirth, or the death of a same-sex partner or spouse. In these cases, the individual might delay his or her grief response or feel it necessary to mourn alone/privately.

Traumatic grief can occur when a death takes place violently, unexpectedly, or causes the loss of someone who dies "before his or her time," such as an infant, child, murder or accident victim, someone stricken with a terminal illness/disease, etc. Sudden or traumatic grief can lead to exaggerated reactions and even post-traumatic stress disorder.

Again, it is important to emphasize that anyone experiencing delayed, disenfranchised, or traumatic grief will not necessarily also deal with complicated grief. In many cases, grievers will still process their grief response normally despite these circumstances and without following the particular "stages" of grief. But if in doubt, then you should consider seeking help from a mental health professional.

TREATMENT OF COMPLICATED GRIEF

Treatment of complicated grief focuses on helping people living with the condition to begin their healing process. Bereavement therapy is most commonly used as a treatment option for this condition.

Where complicated grief evolves or is accompanied by another mental health condition, it's also important to treat this condition. For instance, where it's accompanied by depression, antidepressants might also help to relieve symptoms of complicated grief.

Grief is a difficult emotion to experience and in many cases, it's harder to weather the feelings of loss and sadness that accompany it, on your own. Reaching out to friends and family who can understand what you are going through, is something you shouldn't hesitate to do.

If you are the loved one of a person experiencing complicated grief, you can help by helping the bereaved to find the right treatment and therapy for their condition.

The prescription of medication and engagement in counseling has been the most common methods of treating grief. Initially, your doctor may prescribe you medications to help you function more fully. These might include sedatives, antidepressants, or anti-anxiety medications to help you get through the day. In addition, your doctor might prescribe you medication to help you sleep. This treatment area often causes some differences in opinion in the medical field. Some doctors choose not to prescribe medications because they believe they are doing you a disservice in the grieving process. That is, if a doctor prescribes you anti-anxiety pills or sedation pills – you are not truly experiencing the grief in full effect – you are being subdued from it – potentially interfering with the five stages of grief and eventual acceptance of reality.

Counseling is a more solid approach toward grief. Support groups, bereavement groups, or individual counseling can help you work through unresolved grief. This is a beneficial treatment alternative when you find the grief event is creating obstacles in your everyday life.

That is, you are having trouble functioning and need some support to get back on track. This in no way means it "cures" you of your loss, rather, it provides you with coping strategies to help you effectively deal with your grief. The Kubler-Ross Model is a tried and true guideline but there is no right or wrong way to work through your grief and, normally, your personal experience may vary as you work through the grieving process.

If you or a loved one is having a hard time coping with a grief event, seek treatment from a health professional or mental health provider. Call a doctor right away if you experience thoughts of suicide, feelings of detachment for more than two weeks, you experience a sudden behavior change, or believe you are suffering from depression.

A bereavement counselor will encourage you to monitor your grief, to gain a better understanding of where you are at emotionally. Joining a bereavement support group can also help to cope with feelings of loss and sadness you might be feeling. Learning that you are not alone and some people understand and are experiencing the feelings you have can help you feel better. You might also see a psychodynamic therapist. This therapist may help you identify past losses and their connection to your current loss.

Traumatic grief therapy is another treatment option that has proven to be effective for complicated grief. Here a therapist uses behavioral methods and interpersonal techniques to help you overcome your loss. Your doctor will determine the best treatment plan for you. A combination of medication and therapy might be used to treat complicated grief.

CAUSES OF COMPLICATED GRIEF

There is no identifiable cause of complicated grief, but some people might be more at risk of developing the condition than others. Certain risk factors might make a person more susceptible to experiencing the condition, including:

People who experience an unexpected or shocking death of a loved one
People with a history of mental disorders
People with a history of substance abuse
People who experience more than one death within a short period
Not being present when the loss occurred
Witnessing the loss in real-time

Interference with the healing process of normal grief could also cause complicated grief. Some types of loss might also cause complicated grief—for instance, the loss of a child or a person's significant other. Complicated grief has also proven to be more prevalent in older individuals. A 2011 study evaluated grief in 5,741 older adults and found a prevalence of complicated grief in older adults.

WORDS OF CONDOLENCES TO EXPRESS TOWARDS THE BEREAVED

Have you ever wondered what to say to a friend who has just lost a loved one? You can be assured that whether the person is grieving her sister or another family member, she's in a tremendous amount of emotional pain.

It's not easy to find words of comfort for his or her loss, is it? But the fact remains that you should say something to offer your sympathy and show your support to the person.

What you say doesn't have to belong. It's often better if you keep the words short and focus more on the way you say them.

Even a brief statement letting them know you are thinking of them during their time of grief can be comforting when they are deeply mourning. Sometimes just a few words and a hug or hand squeeze can be the most effective thing you can do.

Finding the Right Words

One of the most difficult things for most people to do is to find the right words to say after someone passes away. It's sad enough that someone has died, but no one wants to slip up and say something to make the surviving family members feel worse.

Some people ramble when they're nervous, so concentrate on keeping your conversation brief and focused on what you are there for. The most important thing is to show sympathy and understanding in as few words as possible.

Comfort During a Time of Grief

It might be tempting to avoid talking to the grieving family altogether, but that is not good either. Rather than avoid talking to the survivors, spend some time thinking about the words that will offer the most comfort. Keep their personalities and temperament in mind, and remember that you don't have to ramble on and on. It is best to keep your communication short but comforting.

Your first words of condolence might be at the funeral. Offer your sympathy, hug the person if it is appropriate, and then back away. Then let someone else have a chance to offer condolences.

If the person wants to talk, listen. Sometimes it's best to not say anything but simply be there to show your support. A simple "I am so sorry" may be all that is needed from you.

After you speak to the family members of the deceased, you may join other conversations during the visitation or before the funeral service begins. Keep your tone low and soothing. Avoid starting or participating in a conversation that is less than respectful to the family and close friends of the deceased.

What to Say

If you find yourself at a loss for words at a funeral, you are not alone. Most people are uncomfortable in this situation. Think before you speak so you don't say something you'll later regret.

Here are some examples of what to say:

1. There are no words to tell you how sorry I am. Please know that you are in our thoughts and prayers.

2. I am so sad to hear about your loss. If you feel like talking, please don't hesitate to call me.

3. John brought so much joy to everyone around him. He will be missed by many.

4. My favorite memory of your grandfather was the time we made ice cream in his backyard. He was truly a wonderful man.

5. I am so sorry for your loss. I will always remember Mary and how much she loved you and the rest of your family.

6. I wish I could take away your pain. Just know that I am thinking about you and praying for comfort for you and your family.

7. If there is anything I can do to help, please let me know.

8. Susan was such a shining light in so many people's lives. We will all miss her terribly. Please know that I will be here for you when you need to talk.

9. I can't even begin to express how my heart aches for you. You will be in my thoughts and prayers.

10. George was such a generous person. We will all miss him, but his legacy will live on through all the great work he did.

11. I'll miss Tom's kind words and sweet smile. Please know that I'll be praying for you and your family.

These words can be spoken before and after the funeral, and you may use them in a sympathy card. What you don't want to do is try to explain a reason for the person's death or act as though the deceased or the family is better off. Even if the person who died suffered for weeks, months, or years, those close to him or her will feel the pain that can't be washed away by explanations.

OVERCOMING

Losing a loved one can be a highly charged and very traumatic time. Though coping with loss can be a deeply personal experience, there are a few basic and universal steps to the bereavement and grief process. Knowing these steps can help you to work through your grief over the loss of a loved one. The pain of grief can often cause you to want to withdraw from others and retreat into your shell. But having the face-to-face support of other people is vital to healing from loss. Even if you're not comfortable talking about your feelings under normal circumstances, it's important to express them when you're grieving. While sharing your loss can make the burden of grief easier to carry, that doesn't mean that every time you interact with friends and family, you need to talk about your loss. Comfort can also come from just being around others who care about you. The key is not to isolate yourself.

Allow the feelings

Coping with the loss of a loved one brings up almost every emotion imaginable. There are times when more than one emotion seems to take hold at once, and you may feel as if you're "going crazy." It's natural to feel this way, as it's normal to experience several different feelings.

Gently remind yourself in your time of bereavement and grief that your feelings are yours, and they are well within the norm. It's important to your process to understand that there is no "right" or "wrong" when it comes to your feelings about losing a loved one.

You may experience a wide range of emotions from sadness, anger, or even exhaustion. All of these feelings are normal and it's important to recognize when you are feeling this way. If you feel stuck or overwhelmed by these emotions, it may be helpful to talk with a licensed psychologist or other mental health professionals who can help you cope with your feelings and find ways to get back on track.

Gather support

While there may be times as you are coping with loss when you'll wish to be alone, it's important to gather a support group around you for those times when you might need them. Friends, family, a minister or rabbi, and perhaps a therapist are all people who can and should be accessed during your grief process. These individuals can be a source of emotional support as well as physical needs if required.

Engaging in support groups can be helpful too. There are local support groups as well as online support groups.

You can connect to others in the group who have gone through or are going through similar losses. They can direct you to further resources as well.

Support groups can also become a safe space where you can express yourself without feeling judged or pressured if you feel that might be the case when talking to somebody else.

Family members, friends, social support groups, and your faith community are all good options to help you work through your grief. You may be able to find a support group focused on a particular type of loss, such as the death of a spouse or a child. Ask your doctor to recommend local resources. The death of a loved one often leaves a large hole in the life of the survivor that can be, at least temporarily, occupied by a support team
.
If you think you may be interested in going to a grief support group, ask a parent, school counselor, or religious leader how to find one. You don't have to be alone with your feelings or your pain.

Grief can feel very lonely, even when you have loved ones around. Sharing your sorrow with others who have experienced similar losses can help.

Allow the grieving process

Bereavement and grief is a process. It's important to know that every person has their way of coping with loss. You cannot put a time limit on your grief. You must allow yourself to experience the stages of grief as they come up.

Each stage is unique and is not necessarily experienced in order. Stages may also be revisited. These stages are:

Denial: Your experience is incomprehensible, initially. You find it impossible to believe the loss of your loved one is real, and you may be numb from the experience.

Anger: As the truth of the situation begins to take hold, it's normal to feel anger and rage. This anger may be directed at yourself, the loved one for leaving you, doctors for not healing your loved one, or even at God.

Bargaining: It's not unusual for survivors to cope with loss by trying to negotiate, usually with their higher power. Don't be surprised if you find yourself trying to make an “if only” deal with God.

Depression: The overwhelming sadness you feel is normal, and in most cases will not last forever. It's common to feel as if life will never be the same.

Acceptance: While this final stage of bereavement and grief is called “acceptance,” this refers to coming to terms with the finality of the loss and moving forward with your life. It does not mean that, from time to time, you may not revisit some of the stages listed above, but rather that the pain of your loss will become more manageable.

Embrace life

While the pain of your loss is real and must be felt, there will come a time when you must begin to live your own life again. By working through overcoming the death of a loved one, you will come to a place of accepting death as a reality. You will find yourself able to move forward and embrace your life without your loved one by your side.

Your process through bereavement and grief is your own. Everyone responds differently to coping with loss. Above all, be kind to yourself and know that you will wake one day and find the pain is less, and life can go on.

Preserve memories

Create a memorial or tribute to the person who died by planting a tree or garden, or fittingly honor the person, like taking part in a charity run or walk.

Make a memory box or folder that has reminders of the person who has died. Include mementos, photos, quotes, or whatever you choose. If you want, write a letter to the person. In it, you might want to include your feelings, things you want to say, or perhaps thank your loved one for being a part of your life. Anniversaries of a lost loved one can be a difficult time for friends and family, but they can also be a time for remembrance and honoring them. It may be that you decide to collect donations to a favorite charity of the deceased, passing on a family name to a baby, or planting a garden in memory. What you choose is up to you, as long as it allows you to honor that unique relationship in a way that feels right to you.

Many people find that specific actions can help honor a deceased parent and offer a measure of comfort.

You might consider:

creating a small home memorial with photos and mementos;
planting their favorite tree or flower in your backyard
adopting their pet or plants;
continuing work they found meaningful, like volunteering or another community service;
donating to their preferred charity or organization

Friends and family

Talking with friends or relatives might give you a sense of relief.

Verbally expressing how you feel can sometimes release some of the inner turmoil you might be experiencing.

Sometimes you might not feel like talking but instead prefer to have silent company.

Expressing your needs to others can allow them to help you in the way you feel is best for your situation.

Now is the time to lean on the people who care about you, even if you take pride in being strong and self-sufficient. Rather than avoiding them, draw friends and loved ones close, spend time together face to face, and accept the assistance that's offered. Often, people want to help but don't know how, so tell them what you need—whether it's a shoulder to cry on, help with funeral arrangements, or just someone to hang out with. If you don't feel you have anyone you can regularly connect with in person, it's never too late to build new friendships.

Talk about it when you can

Some people find it helpful to tell the story of their loss or talk about their feelings. But sometimes a person doesn't feel like talking about a loss, and that's OK, too. No one should feel pressured to talk.

Even if you don't feel like talking, find ways to express your emotions and thoughts. Start writing in a journal about the memories you have of the person you lost and how you're feeling since the loss. Or write a song, poem, or tribute about your loved one. You can do this privately or share it with others.

Talk about the death of your loved one with friends or colleagues to help you understand what happened and remember your friend or family member. Avoidance can lead to isolation and will disrupt the healing process with your support systems.

Mental health professionals

Grief counseling and therapy are two ways to work with a mental health professional who might support your process.

If you have insurance, call your insurer to determine whether this grief counseling is covered under your policy and, if so, under which conditions.

If your insurance doesn’t cover counseling sessions, your primary care doctor might be able to offer some support or guidance.

If you don’t have health insurance or aren’t covered for this service, you could try searching for a local organization that provides grief counseling at a low or no charge.

If your grief feels like too much to bear, find a mental health professional with experience in grief counseling. An experienced therapist can help you work through intense emotions and overcome obstacles to your grieving.

Many national mental health organizations, like the National Alliance on Mental Illness (NAMI), have local or regional chapters. Calling them directly might give you access to some of this information and their specific grief support services.

CONCLUSION

The potential negative effects of a grief reaction can be significant. For example, research shows that about 40% of bereaved people will suffer from some form of anxiety disorder in the first year after the death of a loved one, and there can be up to a 70% increase in death risk of the surviving spouse within the first six months after the death of his or her partner. For these reasons, questionnaires that assess how much stress a person is experiencing usually place the loss of a loved one at the top of the list of the most serious stresses to endure.

When considering the death of a loved one, the effects of losing a pet should not be minimized. Pets are often considered another member of the family, and therefore their loss is grieved as well. Deciding to euthanize (painlessly put to death) the family pet once a family works with their veterinarian to determine that the pet is suffering as a result of their age, specific illness, and/or general declining health can add stress to the bereavement process by leaving family members feeling guilty initially, but if done properly, can help families understand that they spared their beloved pet unnecessary suffering.

In addition to grief as an initial reaction to loss, the process can be aggravated by events that remind the bereaved individuals of their loved ones or the circumstances surrounding their loss. Such events are often referred to as grief triggers. Father's Day or the beginning of the school year may cause the parent who has lost a child (or a child who has lost a parent) to feel distraught. A shared song, television show, or activity can cause anguish by reminding the widower of the wife he lost or the child of the grandparent who is no longer living.

The risk factors for experiencing more serious symptoms of grief for a longer period can be related to the physical and emotional health of the survivor before the loss, the relationship between the bereaved and their loved one, as well as to the nature of the death. For example, it is not uncommon for surviving loved ones who had a contentious or strained relationship, or otherwise unresolved issues with the deceased to suffer severe feelings of sorrow. Parents who have lost their children are at a significantly higher risk of divorce compared to couples who have not. They are also at increased risk for a decline in emotional health, including being psychiatrically hospitalized following the loss. This is a particular risk for mothers who have lost a child.

Bereaved individuals who have experienced an unexpected or violent death of a loved one may be at greater risk for suffering from mental disorders like major depression, posttraumatic stress disorder (PTSD), or complicated grief. According to the Diagnostic and Statistical Manual of Mental Disorders (DSM-5), the accepted diagnostic reference for mental health afflictions, major depression is a psychiatric disorder characterized by sadness and/or irritability that lasts at least two weeks in a row and is accompanied by several other symptoms, like problems with sleep, appetite, weight, concentration, or energy level and may also lead to the sufferer experiencing unjustified guilt, losing interest in activities he or she used to enjoy, or thoughts of wanting to kill themselves or someone else.

Some other things that must be done to cope with grieve are:

Maintain a healthy diet.

Stress triggers cravings for sugar and fat, which is why you reach for feel-good, high-calorie, and high-fat processed food. Yet these foods can make you feel worse. Instead, focus on keeping up a well-balanced diet. That means eating plenty of vegetables, fruits, and lean proteins, and drinking plenty of water.

Follow good sleep hygiene.

Grief is emotionally exhausting. After a loss, people often find that their sleep is disrupted — they have trouble falling asleep, wake up in the middle of the night, or sleep too much. "Going to bed at regular hours, following a bedtime routine, and avoiding caffeine and alcohol in the evening helps with more restful sleep,".

Get moving.

A simple daily walk can help ease depression, agitation, and sorrow related to grief. It is often difficult to find the energy to exercise, so if you lack motivation, enlist a workout buddy or join an exercise group.

Keep tabs on your health.

It's easy to ignore your general health when grieving. This includes skipping doctor visits and forgetting to take your medications. "Schedule all exams for the coming year, so you don't miss them, and set timers on your phone or computer to help remind you to take your medications as scheduled, or ask a friend or family member to assist by checking in with you daily,".

Take on new responsibilities.

The loss of a spouse or family member may mean you have to take over certain routine jobs. For example, you now may be in charge of the cooking, general house upkeep, or organizing financial records. While these tasks can be additional stressors, Dr. Bui suggests turning them into a positive experience. "Taking on a new responsibility can keep your mind focused on a task and distract you from your grief,".

Reach out to your social circle.
While it can be painful to see people, it is important to maintain connections with others. "This reminds you that you are not alone, and even if you feel isolated, there may be family members, friends, or even neighbors who can give a supportive hand," says Dr. Bui. Set up a weekly get-together for lunch or coffee, or invite people over for a monthly potluck. Or just make an effort to communicate with someone every day, either by phone or email.

I am busy going through the stages of grieve but I will forever miss my son. His advice, his voice, his heart, his love will always stay with me. I will always long for him. Religious people had so much to say. Instead of helping they tried to move me towards blame. They almost felt happy about my pain. Most people did not understand what I was going through and could not comprehend the depth of pain, and sorrow I was in;

except for a handful of friends. The pain of losing my beloved son had changed me forever.

I blamed God and fought Him until I realized that He is now taking care of my Son. Our connection is stronger because of God for my son lives in His Presence. Religion does not understand that God can handle humans at their worst because He is God.

Bibliography

There are no sources in the current document.

www.ingramcontent.com/pod-product-compliance
Lightning Source LLC
LaVergne TN
LVHW020652100826
845148LV00012B/2446

* 9 7 8 0 6 2 0 9 4 0 9 2 4 *